Happy 3rd Birthday
Rachael

Lots of love

CHARLOTTE

J. Calvin

Little Fish, Lost

by NANCY VAN LAAN

illustrated by JANE CONTEH-MORGAN

ALADDIN PAPERBACKS

New York   London   Toronto   Sydney   Singapore

Little Fish lost his mother,
where was she, where was she?
Little Fish lost his mother, yes, he did.

Look look here. Look look there.
Little Fish looked everywhere,
but his mother, no, no, no, was not there.

As he swam all around,
up, up, up, down, down, down,
many fish, Little Fish saw.

Striped fish,

freckled fish,

whiskered fish,

puffy fish,

but his mother, no, no no, was not there.

To the top he swam, looking 'round,
where he saw other mothers, yes, he did.

Okapi, sipping water,
sluppa-sup, with its young,

Hippo bathing baby,
splish-a-splash, having fun,

Cheetah sprawling, scrub-a-scrub, cleaned its cub,

but *his* mother no, no, no, was not there.

Little Fish missed his mother,
where was she, where was she?
Little Fish missed his mother, yes, he did.

In the shallows, step-a-step,
was Jocana with her chick.

And in reeds with stalks, very thick,
was Spoonbill, each leg like a stick.

Little Fish whished away, tail a-flick!

Little Fish wanted his mother,
where was she, where was she?
Little Fish wanted his mother, yes, he did.

At the edge of the pond, tippa-taw, prowled Genet.
When she drank, lippa lap,
Little Fish's tail went SLAP!

CLAP! went Crawfish
on the bottom, snappa-snap.

Beetle scooped a tunnel, digga dig.

When turtle hurtled down, Little Fish spun around.

Then off he raced, zigga-zig.

Little Fish needed his mother,
where was she, where was she?
Little Fish needed his mother, yes, he did.

So Little Fish strayed way a-way to the deep, dark middle,
where a fish as big as it could be,
whipped its tail, woosh woosh,
stretched its mouth, gullumph gullumph,

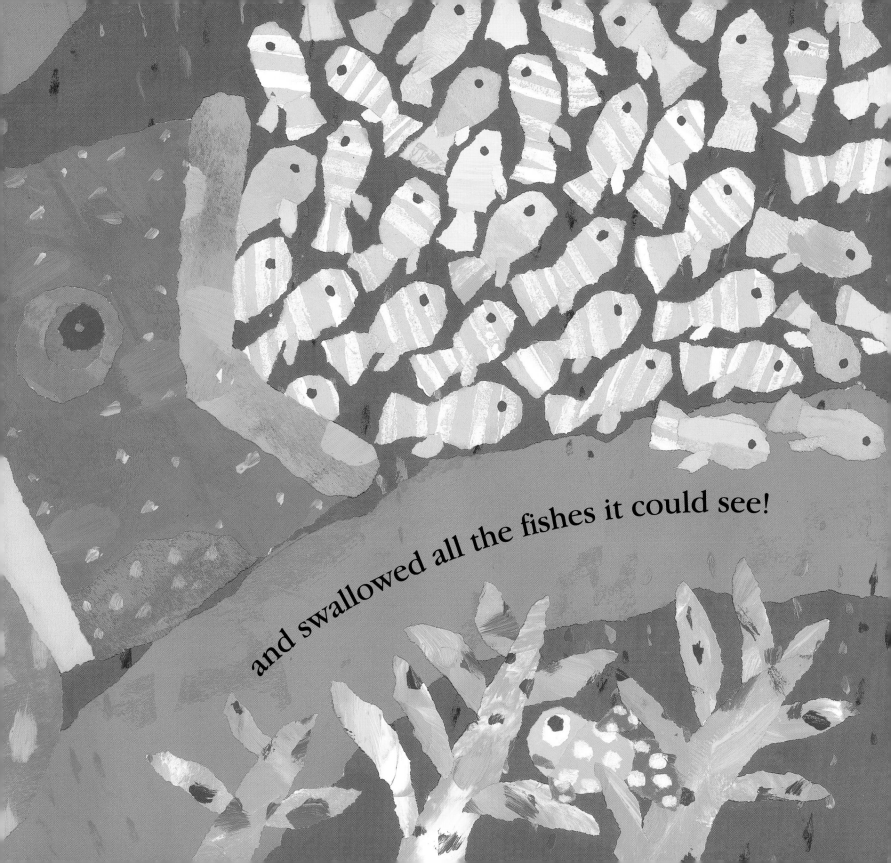

and swallowed all the fishes it could see!

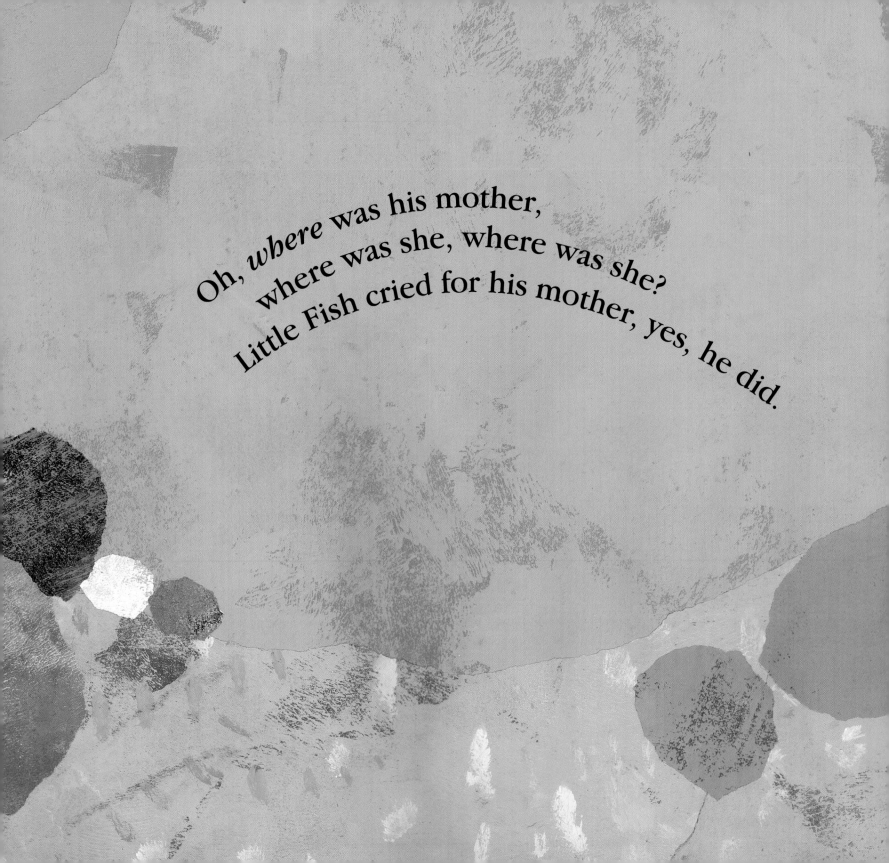

Oh, *where* was his mother,
where was she, where was she?
Little Fish cried for his mother, yes, he did.

Then all alone,
he slipped between two stones,
tail and fin tucked in, thinny thin.

It was there, right there, Little Fish found his mother, who wondered where, where, where had *he* been!

Was he happy, was he?

Was she happy,
was she?

Through reeds, hidden deep,
side by side, swim swim leap.

Little Fish found his mother,

yes,
he did!

For my good friend Jane, who always knows where I am
—N. V. L.
For my four little fish: Bundu, Obai, Sorie, Amie
—J. C-M.

First Aladdin Paperbacks edition August 2001
Text copyright © 1998 by Nancy Van Laan
Illustrations © 1998 by Jane Conteh-Morgan
Aladdin Paperbacks
An imprint of Simon & Schuster
Children's Publishing Division
1230 Avenue of the Americas
New York, NY 10020
Also available in an Atheneum Books for Young Readers hardcover edition
Designed by Ann Bobco
The text for this book was set in Garamond ITC.
The illustrations were rendered in collage.
Printed and bound in Hong Kong

10 9 8 7 6 5 4 3 2 1

The Library of Congress has cataloged the hardcover edition as follows:
Van Laan, Nancy.
Little Fish, lost / by Nancy Van Laan ;
illustrated by Jane Conteh-Morgan.—1st ed.
p.   cm.
"An Anne Schwartz book."
Summary: Little Fish loses his mother in an African pond and searches everywhere
for her, seeing all kinds of animals in the process.
ISBN: 0-689-81331-7 (hc.)
[1. Fishes—Fiction. 2. Animals—Fiction. 3. Zoology—Africa—Fiction.
4. Africa—Fiction. 5. Mother and child—Fiction. 6. Stories in rhyme.]
I. Conteh-Morgan, Jane, ill. II. Title.
PZ8.3.V47Li 1998
[E]—dc20
96-26344
ISBN: 0-689-84372-0 (Aladdin pbk.)